Popular Rock Superstars of Yesterday and Today
POP ROCK

AC/DC	Elton John
Aerosmith	The Grateful Dead
The Allman Brothers Band	Led Zeppelin
The Beatles	Lynyrd Skynyrd
Billy Joel	Pink Floyd
Bob Marley and the Wailers	Queen
Bruce Springsteen	The Rolling Stones
The Doors	U2
	The Who

Pink Floyd

Herman Edward

Mason Crest Publishers

Pink Floyd

FRONTIS Syd Barrett, Nick Mason, Rick Wright, and Roger Waters (left to right), were the original members of one of the biggest bands in rock history—Pink Floyd.

Produced by 21st Century Publishing and Communications, Inc.

Editorial by Harding House Publishing Services, Inc.

MASON CREST PUBLISHERS INC.
370 Reed Road
Broomall, Pennsylvania 19008
(866) MCP-BOOK (toll free)
www.masoncrest.com

Printed in the United States.

First Printing

9 8 7 6 5 4 3 2 1

Library of Congress Cataloging-in-Publication Data

Edward, Herman.
    Pink Floyd / Herman Edward.
       p. cm. — (Popular rock superstars of yesterday and today)
    Includes bibliographical references and index.
    Hardback edition: ISBN-13: 978-1-4222-0214-2
    Paperback edition: ISBN-13: 978-1-4222-0313-2
  1. Pink Floyd (Musical group)—Juvenile literature. 2. Rock musicians—England—Biography—Juvenile literature. I. Title.
ML3930.P47 E48 2008
782.42166092'2—dc22
[B]   2007015905

Publisher's notes:

- All quotations in this book come from original sources, and contain the spelling and grammatical inconsistencies of the original text.

- The Web sites mentioned in this book were active at the time of publication. The publisher is not responsible for Web sites that have changed their addresses or discontinued operation since the date of publication. The publisher will review and update the Web site addresses each time the book is reprinted.

CONTENTS

Rock 'n' Roll Timeline

1951
"Rocket 88," considered by many to be the first rock single, is released by Ike Turner.

1952
DJ Alan Freed coins and popularizes the term "Rock and Roll," proclaims himself the "Father of Rock and Roll," and declares, "Rock and Roll is a river of music that has absorbed many streams: rhythm and blues, jazz, rag time, cowboy songs, country songs, folk songs. All have contributed to the Big Beat."

1955
"Rock Around the Clock" by Bill Haley & His Comets is released; it tops the U.S. charts and becomes wildly popular in Britain, Australia, and Germany.

1967
The Monterey Pop Festival in California kicks off open air rock concerts.

1965
The psychedelic rock band, the Grateful Dead, is formed in San Francisco.

1969
The Woodstock Music and Arts Festival attracts a huge crowd to rural upstate New York.

1969
Tommy, the first rock opera, is released by British rock band The Who.

1970
The Beatles break up.

1971
Jim Morrison, lead singer of The Doors, dies in Paris.

1971
Duane Allman, lead guitarist of the Allman Brothers Band, dies.

1950s 1960s 1970s

1957
Bill Haley tours Europe.

1957
Jerry Lee Lewis and Buddy Holly become the first rock musicians to tour Australia.

1954
Elvis Presley releases the extremely popular single "That's All Right (Mama)."

1961
The first Grammy for Best Rock 'n' Roll Recording is awarded to Chubby Checker for *Let's Twist Again*.

1964
The Beatles make their first visit to America, setting off the British Invasion.

1969
A rock concert held at Altamont Speedway in California is marred by violence.

1969
The Rolling Stones tour America as "The Greatest Rock and Roll Band in the World."

1973
Rolling Stone magazine names Annie Leibovitz chief photographer and "rock 'n' roll photographer;" she follows and photographs rockers Mick Jagger, John Lennon, and others.

1974
Sheer Heart Attack by the British rock band Queen becomes an international success.

1974
"Sweet Home Alabama" by Southern rock band Lynyrd Skynyrd is released and becomes an American anthem.

1987
Billy Joel becomes the first American rock star to perform in the Soviet Union since the construction of the Berlin Wall.

2005
Led Zeppelin is ranked #1 on VH1's list of the 100 Greatest Artists of Hard Rock.

1985
Rock stars perform at Live Aid, a benefit concert to raise money to fight Ethiopian famine.

2005
Many rock groups participate in Live 8, a series of concerts to raise awareness of extreme poverty in Africa.

2003
Led Zeppelin's "Stairway to Heaven" is inducted into the Grammy Hall of Fame.

1980
John Lennon of the Beatles is murdered in New York City.

2000s
Aerosmith's album sales reach 140 million worldwide and the group becomes the bestselling American hard rock band of all time.

1975
Tommy, the movie, is released.

2007
Billy Joel become the first person to sing the National Anthem before two Super Bowls.

1975
Time magazine features Bruce Springsteen on its cover as "Rock's New Sensation."

1995
The Rock and Roll Hall of Fame and Museum opens in Cleveland, Ohio.

1970s 1980s 1990s 2000s

1979
Pink Floyd's *The Wall* is released.

1991
Freddie Mercury, lead vocalist of the British rock group Queen, dies of AIDS.

2004
Elton John receives a Kennedy Center Honor.

1979
The first Grammy for Best Rock Vocal Performance by a Duo or Group is awarded to The Eagles.

2004
Rolling Stone Magazine ranks The Beatles #1 of the 100 Greatest Artists of All Time, and Bob Dylan #2.

1986
The Rolling Stones receive a Grammy Lifetime Achievement Award.

1981
MTV goes on the air.

2006
U2 wins five more Grammys, for a total of 22—the most of any rock artist or group.

1986
The first Rock and Roll Hall of Fame induction ceremony is held; Chuck Berry, Little Richard, Ray Charles, Elvis Presley, and James Brown, are among the first inductees.

1981
For Those About to Rock We Salute You by Australian rock band AC/DC becomes the first hard rock album to reach #1 in the U.S.

2006
Bob Dylan, at age 65, releases *Modern Times* which immediately rises to #1 in the U.S.

Live 8 brought together some of rock's biggest bands, past and present, including Dave Gilmour, Roger Waters, Nick Mason, and Rick Wright (left to right). For the first time in more than twenty years, Pink Floyd performed together at the July 2, 2005, concert. Fans all over the world were thrilled. Hopes of a real reunion surfaced—again.

Together Again for Justice

People in the audience were getting antsy. Many believed they would never see it happen. Others had always been sure it would happen if they were just patient. Still others in the audience had hoped they'd be there to witness it but had had doubts as twenty-four years passed. Finally, here it was: Pink Floyd was on stage—with Roger Waters.

The last time Roger had joined David Gilmour, Nick Mason, and Rick Wright for a Pink Floyd performance was on June 17, 1981, for a concert at London's Earls Court. Now, on July 2, 2005, the four were together again, this time to help people a continent away.

Live 8

In 1984, Bob Geldof of the Irish rock band Boomtown Rats and Midge Ure worked together to bring the famine in the African country of Ethiopia to the attention of rock fans all over the world. British musicians got together in a London recording studio to record "Do They Know It's Christmas." The single raised millions for Ethiopian famine relief. The following year, the duo put together Live Aid, a multi-**venue** series of concerts that again raised money to help those affected by the Ethiopian famine.

Now, twenty years after Live Aid, Bob Geldof and Midge Ure were back with another series of concerts to help those in Africa. This time, though, the purpose wasn't quite the same. Instead of money, Bob and Midge wanted to raise awareness of the problems massive amounts of debt was causing **third-world** countries, especially those on the continent of Africa. The Group of 8 (G8), the leaders of the most prosperous countries in the world, was about to meet, and concert organizers wanted to catch their attention, as well as spur rock fans to take action and contact their countries' representatives. Just as they had with Live Aid, the organizers turned to some of the biggest names in rock—including Pink Floyd.

But would Pink Floyd agree to the project? After all, Roger hadn't left the group on the friendliest of terms. According to David Gilmour in an interview with the BBC:

> **"Like most people I want to do everything I can to persuade the G8 leaders to make huge commitments to the relief of poverty and increased aid to the third world. Any squabbles Roger and the band have had in the past are so petty in this context, and if reforming for this concert will help focus attention, then it's got to be worthwhile."**

Pink Floyd at Live 8

Live 8 concerts took place in Philadelphia, London, Berlin, Rome, Paris, as well as in Japan, South Africa, and Canada. Pink Floyd joined such artists as Madonna, REM, U2, Paul McCartney, Elton John, Coldplay, and Robbie Williams at the concert in London's Hyde Park.

The re-formed band played some of its biggest hits: "Speak to Me," "Money," "Breathe," and "Comfortably Numb." Roger addressed the

LIVE FROM HYDE PARK, LONDON
JULY 2, 2005

LIVE 8

PINK FLOYD

THE REUNION CONCERT

Live 8 wasn't about money; it was about raising awareness of a good cause. But it also raised hopes for a Pink Floyd reunion tour. The band's performance had been phenomenal, and the guys seemed to enjoy playing together again. For now, though, fans will have to be contented with a DVD of the group's performance.

enthusiastic crowd during the introduction to another of the group's hits, "Wish You Were Here":

"It's actually quite emotional standing up here with these three guys after all these years. Standing to be counted with the rest of you. Anyway, we're doing this for everyone who's not here, but particularly, of course, for Syd."

By Syd, Roger meant Syd Barrett, one of the group's original members, who left the group in 1968.

Joining Roger, David, Nick, and Rick were Tim Renwick on guitar, Jon Carin on keyboards and backup vocals, Dick Parry on saxophone, and backup singer Carol Kenyon. Many of them had played with Pink Floyd or with the group's members on solo projects after the group called it quits.

On July 2, 2005, there were two places for music lovers to be—at one of the Live 8 concert venues or watching the concerts on television. The biggest names performed— Madonna, U2, Coldplay, Pink Floyd. The concerts provided individuals a chance to enjoy an unforgettable musical trip and learn something about the world along the way.

Flashes from the Past

Fans in the audience and watching at home on television were treated to a pictorial walk down memory lane during Pink Floyd's performance. Well, it was memory lane for some, but not everyone rockin' to the group that day was old enough to remember the group. To them, the performance was new and exciting.

Highlights from Pink Floyd's recording past were flashed on the big-screen backdrop while the group played. The famous flying pig was shown during "Breathe," and the Pink Floyd Wall was featured when the guys played "Comfortably Numb." To remind everyone why Pink Floyd had joined the other musicians at Live 8, the words "Make Poverty History" were flashed on the screen as well.

When the last song had been sung and the last chord struck, David thanked the fans and turned to walk offstage, but Roger called him back to where he and the others were. Then, completely unexpected to everyone, David, Roger, Nick, and Rick had a group hug. Those who knew the band's history, especially the hard feelings when Roger left, couldn't believe their eyes. Most of the highlight films of the concert feature that scene.

The reunion concert spurred hopes in the fans that the group would reunite for good. Pink Floyd's fans were loyal, and they would have loved *their* band to re-form and begin producing the music they missed. And as a result of Live 8, Pink Floyd had a new set of fans. Fans all over the world hoped that the concert would help the group find its way back to the days when all was good for the band once known by the unlikely name Tea Set.

The sixties were an exciting time in music, especially in London. Among the many groups that formed then was Pink Floyd—Syd Barrett, Nick Mason, Rick Wright, and Roger Waters (left to right). But Pink Floyd's musical influence didn't stop in the 1960s. It continues to influence groups today, more than forty years after the group began.

Becoming Pink Floyd

Many bands go through a variety of names before settling on *the* one. That was certainly true for the group that eventually became Pink Floyd. When Bob Klose, Roger Waters, Nick Mason, and Rick Wright got together with some other musicians in 1964, the group's name changed as often as one changes socks.

One Too Many Tea Sets

First, the group was called Sigma 6. Then it was the Megga Deaths, the Screaming Abdabs, and then just the Abdabs (apparently they weren't screaming anymore). Having the right name was the least of the group's problems, and it broke up not long after it began. Bob, Roger, Nick, and Rick weren't ready to call it quits, though. They enjoyed playing together, so they began a new band, Tea Set. (In some references, the group's name is spelled T Set.) Chris Dennis joined the group to provide lead vocals. Syd Barrett came onboard in 1965 as a guitarist and to provide vocals. To take advantage of Syd's guitar talents, Roger agreed to move to bass. When Chris left the group after a brief time, the vocalist duties fell to Syd.

Bob, Roger, Nick, Rick, and Syd were now known as Tea Set. Before long, however, they discovered they weren't the only Tea Set playing the London music scene. One night the guys showed up for a gig and found—much to their surprise—that another group called Tea Set was scheduled to perform that night as well.

So the guys again found themselves in search of a name. Syd liked the name "The Pink Floyd Sound." The name was an **homage** to American bluesmen Pinkney "Pink" Anderson and Floyd Council. According to Pink Floyd history, Syd read about the two on **liner notes** for a 1962 album by Blind Boy Fuller. The guys settled on The Pink Floyd Sound, but Sound didn't last. However, for many years, the group continued to use "The" as an official part of its name.

Early Pink Floyd

The group had now agreed on a name, so it was time to concentrate on the music. At first, the group played covers, "redos" of songs that had already been recorded by someone else. The group's preference was for rhythm and blues sounds, and that is where they searched for their songs.

One of their best known early covers was "Louie, Louie." The song, written by Richard Berry and first released in 1955, has a legend all its own. According to the Web site www.louielouie.net:

"Fact: With the exception of Paul McCartney's 'Yesterday,' it's been covered more times than any other pop song (over 1,000 versions and counting).

Fact: KFJC, a college radio station in Los Altos Hills, California, once played it for 63 hours straight without repeating the same recording twice, receiving unprecedented coverage in the *Wall Street Journal, Entertainment Tonight, Playboy* magazine and various other international media sources.

Like many new bands, Pink Floyd began by doing covers of other artists' songs. But like new bands who want to make a major mark on the music scene, Pink Floyd set out to create a sound uniquely their own. And that they did, eventually becoming rock legends and the inspiration to many other musicians.

Fact: It was the subject of obscenity investigations by the FBI and the FCC, culminating in an airwave ban in the state of Indiana. ❞

The best-known recording of "Louie, Louie" was by the Kingsmen in 1963.

Bob Klose (left) was an early member of Pink Floyd, but wasn't a part of the Pink Floyd that made it big. Bob's idea of what the band should play didn't mesh with those of the other guys. So he left the group. But don't feel sorry for him—he became very well known practicing another of his loves, photography.

Nick, Roger, Rick, Bob, and Syd didn't just want to do something someone else had done; they were too talented for that. So they did what they could to make their version of the song unique, even unforgettable. In some cases they added guitar solos that seemed to go on forever. Before long, Pink Floyd interpreted the songs with the psychedelic flavor for which they would become famous. The sounds and light shows would touch almost all the listeners' senses and make the songs the group's own.

Becoming Four

On October 12, 1965, the city of London was introduced to Pink Floyd when Roger, Rick, Nick, Bob, and Syd were booked to play under that name for the first time. The guys played at the Countdown Club, which wasn't a huge venue but did provide the group with an appreciative audience. The group's set still featured primarily rhythm and blues covers. The band soon gained a following and became regulars at small clubs around London.

Although things were looking up for the group, not everyone was happy. Bob Klose was one of those who weren't pleased with the way the group appeared to be headed. Bob had a different focus from other band members. He was a serious student. Even his music preferences were different from those of the other members of Pink Floyd. He shared the others' interest in rhythm and blues, but Bob was mostly interested in jazz. And he wasn't pleased with the sounds Syd was encouraging for the band. Syd's idea to make the band's sound unique was to create a psychedelic and more pop sound to Pink Floyd's music. Bob wanted to keep its bluesy overtones. Before long, it became clear that Bob wasn't going to be able to sway the guys over to his side.

Bob also had another interest he wanted to pursue. He had proven himself to be a very talented photographer. For a while, Bob wasn't sure he wanted to be a musician; perhaps he should become a photographer. So, even before Pink Floyd could cut a record, and just when they were experiencing the beginning of success, Bob decided to leave the group. He continued to do some performing, but he also established himself as a photographer.

Now with only four members, Pink Floyd began its climb to the top of the rock world.

Pulsating and flashing lights. Wild and distorted images and sounds. Colors, colors, and more colors. These were all characteristics of psychedelic rock, one of the hot trends in music during the 1960s. But so were mind-altering drugs, and their effects could last long after the music—and be very life-altering as well.

Psychedelia Comes to the U.K.

With one less member, Pink Floyd had to make adjustments in who would do what. Syd sang leads and played the guitar. Roger sang backup and played bass. Nick was responsible for all the percussion instruments, and Rick moved over to play keyboards and provide some backup vocals as well. This was the lineup for the next few years.

Developing a Sound

With a set lineup, it was time to work on the sound. Before long, Syd (his actual name was Roger Keith Barrett) established himself as the band's leader. Though he had exhibited leadership tendencies from the time he joined the group—even playing the major role in naming the group—he took more control after Bob left the group. Syd was a talented songwriter with definite ideas about the direction he wanted Pink Floyd to take. He wasn't happy that the group was concentrating on covers of American songs. Syd felt they were too much like the Rolling Stones, the Kinks, and the Yardbirds, other bands active in Britain at the time.

What Pink Floyd needed was some way to make the group and its music stand out from the other bands. Rock seemed to be everywhere in the mid- to late 1960s, and being good just wasn't enough to become successful. There were a lot of good bands, and Syd and the guys knew they wanted to be more than just another good band.

Syd was the group's primary songwriter, and he worked to write songs that would help the group make a name for itself. He looked at what the other groups were doing. And he examined what was popular in the United States as well as in Britain. That's when he hit on what he felt was the key to Pink Floyd success—psychedelic rock.

Psychedelic Rock

Rock music changed during the 1960s. One reason for the change was an increased availability of illegal drugs, including those called psychedelics. Psychedelics can produce weird, distorted, wildly colorful images or sounds. Among the most popular of these mind-altering drugs were **cannabis**, **mescaline**, and LSD.

Before long, the drugs, and their effects, found their way into the day's rock 'n' roll music, and psychedelic rock was the result. The Grateful Dead and the Vanilla Fudge were two of the leading psychedelic bands in the United States. In Britain, some of the Beatles' songs fell into the psychedelic rock **genre**. But the two bands that would become **synonymous** with the label were Cream and Pink Floyd.

In February 1966, Pink Floyd played a series of "happenings" at the Marquee Club in London. These concerts were dubbed the Spontaneous **Underground**. In September, the group played a fund-raising concert to benefit Britain's first underground newspaper, the *International Times*. The next month the group played for the paper's launch. The band introduced its lively, hypnotic visual special effects at these shows. When Pink Floyd played at the All Night Rave Pop Op Costume Masque Drag Ball Et All on the opening night of London's famous Roundhouse, they did away with any remaining doubts that the group was like all the others on the London music scene. Syd, Nick, Rick, and Roger had found a way for Pink Floyd to break out of the pack of rock bands.

In the United States, the Grateful Dead, fronted by the legendary Jerry Garcia, was one of the most famous psychedelic bands. Playing to packed venues all across the country, the band often ranked at the top of the highest-grossing tour list. Their dedicated fans—and there were and are millions—called themselves Deadheads.

Earning a Rep

By late 1966, Britain's underground and **counterculture** were gaining in popularity and brought increased interest in Pink Floyd and other psychedelic bands. Just before Christmas 1966, the band played at the first of many shows benefiting the *International Times* at the UFO Club in London. The club became *the* place to play if you were a psychedelic band, and Pink Floyd became the club's house band. Part of a January 1967 Pink Floyd at the UFO performance was shown on Granada Television; this is the first record of a live performance by the group. For a while, Pink Floyd played both the UFO Club and its rival the Roundhouse. Instead of hurting attendance at each club, the cross-appearances brought more and more people into both clubs. The group became the poster child for psychedelic rock.

Pink Floyd was hot, and so was psychedelic music—and clearly, Pink Floyd had played a major role in its popularity. According to the Rock and Roll Hall of Fame,

> **"What George Orwell and Ray Bradbury were to literature, Pink Floyd is to popular music, forging an unsettling but provocative combination of science fiction and social commentary."**

By the mid- to late 1960s, Pink Floyd had made a name for itself as *the* psychedelic band in London. If there was a club that featured psychedelic music, one could be sure that Pink Floyd had, or would, play there. When someone thought of psychedelic rock, the group that immediately popped into mind was Pink Floyd.

And Pink Floyd's move into psychedelic rock had come at the urging of Syd. He had wanted the group to move away from covers, and psychedelic rock was about as far away as it could get. The Rock and Roll Hall of Fame states that

"In their early years, with vocalist, guitarist and songwriter Syd Barrett at the helm, Pink Floyd were the psychedelic Pied Pipers of the 'London underground' scene."

Pink Floyd's unique sound was even catching the attention of the film industry. In December 1966, filmmaker Peter Whitehead asked the group to perform two songs for his film *Tonite Let's All Make Love in London*. After the beginning of the new year, the group laid down "Interstellar Overdrive" and "Nick's Boogie" for the film. Neither was used in the film, but the video of their session was released in 2005.

To the Studio

No matter how good a group is in a gig, eventually it will have to go into the recording studio and cut a record. In 1967, Pink Floyd found itself in a recording studio in Chelsea, ready to cut its first single. That single, "Arnold Layne," hit #20 on the British charts. The song's success came despite the fact that it was banned from many of Britain's radio stations. The song is about a **cross-dresser** who steals women's garments (including underwear) from clotheslines. According to some people, Syd wrote the song about a real person, someone who stole such clothing from the clotheslines of his and Roger's mothers in Cambridge. Whether based on a real-life situation or not, the song's subject was just too "abnormal" to be played on the radio, at least according to the authorities who ran British radio.

A second single was released, "See Emily Play," and it sold even more copies, reaching #6 on the British singles charts. British radio programmers did not have a problem with playing that song on the radio.

On April 5, 1967, Pink Floyd's debut album was released. The title, *Piper at the Gates of Dawn*, was taken from the classic book *Wind in the Willows*. The album was a critical success. In a 1995 article, *Q* magazine stated:

Who could have thought that a song banned from most British radio stations could be the beginning of a music career that would span decades? Pink Floyd's first single, a song about a cross-dresser, beat the odds to reach #20 on the British singles chart. The story may—or may not—be about an incident from Syd's and Roger's childhoods.

❝ *Piper at the Gates of Dawn* is, even counting *Sgt. Pepper* [by the Beatles] possibly the defining moment of English psychedelia and Syd Barrett's magnum opus.**❞**

It was also a commercial success, at least in Britain, where it topped at #6 on the album charts; it only ranked as high as #131 in the United States.

Piper at the Gates of Dawn highlighted Syd's talents as a songwriter and as a guitarist. He wrote or cowrote all but one of the tracks on the album. His lyrics were a mixture of poetry and folklore. His guitar-playing on the album showed his tendency toward experimentation.

He used distortion, feedback, and echo on the album. Syd also played the guitar by sliding a lighter up and down the strings to get an unusual sound.

Live and In Person

Once work in the studio was done, Pink Floyd was out performing for its fans again. They participated in the April 29–April 30, 1967, fund-raising event for the *International News*, held at Alexandra Palace in

With the release of its first album, *Piper at the Gates of Dawn*, Pink Floyd came to the attention of the critics and a bigger group of music lovers. The critics loved the group and its unique sound. So did the British fans. It would take longer before the group found success in the United States.

London. The concerts were a who's who of the rock world, with an audience filled with distinguished actors and artists. Among the musicians who joined Pink Floyd were the Who, Pretty Things, and Soft Machine. In the audience were John Lennon, Yoko Ono, Michael Caine, Julie Christie, and Mick Jagger. Parts of the concert were filmed, but none of Pink Floyd's performance was preserved.

In May 1967, the group performed at the Games for May concert at London's Queen Elizabeth Hall. In 1967, the group would also tour with American superstar Jimi Hendrix. The combination of the well-known Jimi Hendrix and Pink Floyd helped increase the popularity of the group on both sides of the Atlantic Ocean.

On May 14, 1967, Rick, Nick, Roger, and Syd appeared on British television for the first time. The success of "Arnold Layne" brought the group to the attention of the producers of *The Look of the Week*, who invited them to perform. This was the group's first appearance on British television.

One of the hottest music shows on British television was *Top of the Pops*. Most of the top musical groups performed on the series. In July 1967, the shows producers asked Pink Floyd to perform on the show. It was a good opportunity for exposure, but not all members were anxious to appear. According to the Web site Pink-Floyd.org (www.pinkfloyd.org), Syd didn't think he should have to perform on the show. After all, John Lennon didn't appear on *Top of the Pops*. To his bandmates and the group's managers, this attitude was more evidence that something was wrong with Syd.

What's Up With Syd?

Syd always had his own style, his own way of doing things, and sometimes they could be called odd. But by mid-1967, his behavior had gone beyond odd to sometimes troubling. There seemed to be a direct relationship between the group's success and Syd's unusual behavior; as Pink Floyd became more famous, Syd's actions became weirder. But that wasn't the only thing that increased along with Pink Floyd's success—so did Syd's use of LSD.

In November 1967, Pink Floyd came to the United States for the first time. During an interview with the other members of the group, Syd refused to answer questions or lip-synch the songs the group was scheduled to perform. During concerts, Syd would sometimes play

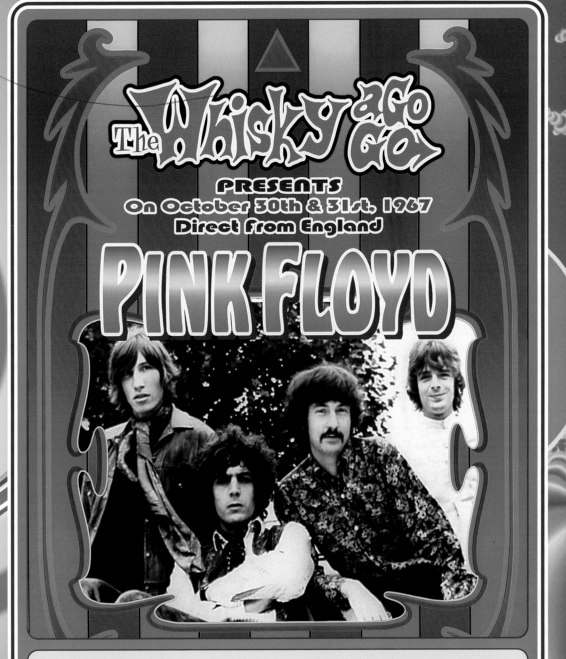

The Whisky a Go Go

PRESENTS

On October 30th & 31st, 1967
Direct From England

PINK FLOYD

In 1967 Pink Floyd came to the United States and to an audience anxious to see the band perform. One of the clubs that hosted the group was the famous Whisky A Go Go. Many of the biggest names in rock music played there at some point in their careers.

With Syd's growing unpredictability and odd behavior, the other members of Pink Floyd went in search of a new guitarist. They found him in David Gilmour. This photo shows the five-member Pink Floyd: (from left) Nick, Syd, Roger, Rick, and David. Before long, Syd left the group, and the band found itself without the songwriter who had brought it success.

the same chord all night long; other times he'd just stand on stage and not do anything at all. During a concert at the famous Fillmore West in San Francisco, Syd systematically detuned his guitar. Another time, before taking the stage for a concert, Syd rubbed a tube of the hair gel Brylcreem into his hair (despite the gel's jingle that claimed "a little dab will do ya"). During the course of the concert, as the stage grew hot from the lights and the performance, the hair cream began to melt, until it ran down Syd's face.

Most fans were unaware that Syd's antics were not planned. Some of his shenanigans were actually very funny, and the audience seemed to enjoy them, thinking they were just part of the show. But his behavior was not funny to the other members of Pink Floyd. They got angry and frustrated with the frontman; finally, in December 1967, the guys made it known they were looking for a guitarist. The guys' intent wasn't to replace Syd; they just wanted to make sure that a guitarist would be available should Syd not be in a condition to perform.

In January 1968, David Gilmour joined the band as guitarist. For a while, the group performed as a five-member band, but Syd performed less and less until David became the full-time guitarist. At first, the guys hoped Syd would still write for the group, but that didn't work out either. Finally, on April 6, 1968, the group sent out a press release announcing that Syd would no longer be a member of Pink Floyd.

The Aftermath

Syd wasn't the only person Pink Floyd lost because of that decision. The guys' management group didn't agree with the decision to cut Syd from the group, and they stayed with Syd. So not only had the group lost the person who had been responsible for much of its success, it also lost the people who had handled the nuts and bolts of being a top rock group.

Even though the group and management had parted ways, Pink Floyd topped the card at the first free Hyde Park concert, organized by its former managers.

Pink Floyd returned to the United States in the summer of 1968 on a tour supporting its new album *A Saucerful of Secrets*. Most of the songs were written by someone other than Syd. The group had officially entered its post-Syd phase.

The guys all liked Syd, but when it became obvious that something "wasn't right," they knew the change was the right thing to do. But would Pink Floyd be able to achieve success without its leader and main songwriter? Yes. Rick, Roger, Nick, and David—left to right, the new Pink Floyd—are shown in a relaxed moment.

Worldwide Success and The Wall

S yd's contributions to Pink Floyd had been many, but in the end, he was a distraction, and his behavior was often an embarrassment to his band mates. Nick, Rick, Roger, and David were anxious to get on with their career. Songwriting and vocals were now shared by Rick, Roger, and David. But that wasn't the only change the band made.

A Change in Style

When Syd was part of the band, it was obvious that he was the group's leader. With his departure, Rick at first seemed to take over that responsibility, but eventually, Roger became Pink Floyd's recognized leader.

The new songs were very different from those that had brought the group its initial fame. Rick, Roger, and David all wrote songs, and their music represented what interested them, not necessarily what was hot in music at the time. Rick's music held on to the psychedelic sound Syd had nurtured, but he emphasized the keyboards, which, of course, he played. David liked the blues, and his songs were dependent on a strong guitar line. As for Roger, he liked jazz songs, and paid particular attention to the lyrics; his songs had to have meaning. Of course, the bass line was featured in most songs he wrote.

Though it took time, the group eventually lost its association with psychedelic music. In an interview with *Guitar* magazine, David talked about what the group tried to do with their music after Syd left:

> **"I like our music to feel three-dimensional. It's about trying to invoke emotions in people, I suppose. You feel larger than life in some sort of way. Let's face it none of us in Pink Floyd are technically brilliant musicians, with great chops who can change rhythms, fifteen or sixteen bars here, there and everywhere. And we're not terribly good at complicated chord structures. A lot of it is just very simple stuff dressed up. We stopped trying to make overtly 'spacey' music and trip people out in that way in the 60's. But that image hangs on and we can't seem to get shot of it."**

A Change in Audience

Another reason Pink Floyd's music changed was because its audience changed. According to Glenn Povey and Ian Russell, authors of *Pink Floyd: In the Flesh: The Complete Performance History*, after Syd left, the group attracted a more "intellectual" crowd. Instead of yelling, screaming, and otherwise carrying on during a song, this audience was more likely to sit still, erupting in approval only after it was certain the last note had been played.

This crowd wasn't interested in a fancy, elaborate light show or wild, hypnotic imagery. Those in the audience were there to hear the music. They weren't interested in musicians trying to **mesmerize** them by using visual effects. So in response to its changing audience, the members of Pink Floyd changed how they spent any profits they had. Instead of buying the most up-to-date and elaborate visual

New member—new sound. Syd and his style preferences had been the group's driving force. But his departure allowed others to come to the front, and from the change, a new sound developed. Pink Floyd's psychedelic days were put behind it; that had been Syd's thing. Now, with new writers and a new sound, worldwide success was finally achieved.

effects, money was put into buying and upgrading the group's sound system. If a concert stop wanted a light show or other fancy visual effects, the promoter or venue had to pick up the tab.

A Mish-Mash

A Saucerful of Secrets, released in 1968, was the only Pink Floyd album not to make the charts in the United States. It hit #9 in Britain, but the critics were neutral about it. Most felt it was uneven, mixing some of the psychedelic rock sounds with songs that reflected more of the "new" Pink Floyd. Whatever the reason for its lack of critical success, the group knew it had to hit a home run with the next one.

The next Pink Floyd project was a soundtrack for the 1969 film _More_. Again critics were not particularly excited about the offering, released as the Pink Floyd album _Music From the Film More_ in July 1969. But again, it reached #9 in Britain. This time, however, the group

Flashy light shows and movie-worthy special effects were put by the wayside by the new Pink Floyd. Oh, it wasn't that the group was against them in principle. Pink Floyd was happy to include them in its concerts, but someone else had to pay for them. The band was spending its money on top-of-the line sound equipment.

found itself back on the U.S. charts, though only at #153. Some of the songs, including "Cymbaline," did become **bootleg** hits.

Ummagumma was released in October 1969, though not in the form it was originally intended. The album was supposed to be a mixture of sounds from "found" noisemakers instead of traditional instruments. But everything seemed to go wrong on the project, and the group gave up that idea. So instead, the double album contains live performances along with solos by group members; each member was allowed one-half of one side of the album for his solo experiment. When released, it became Pink Floyd's most popular album at the time.

Hitting the Top in the United States

It might have looked as though Pink Floyd was never going to make it big in the United States. Its concerts were well attended, and the crowds were enthusiastic, but when it came to recordings, they just

As it had from the beginning, the members of Pink Floyd loved to experiment with their sound. In 1969, the group had its biggest-selling album to date, *Ummagumma*. Each member had a portion of an album for a solo performance. The rest of the album featured live performances by Pink Floyd.

didn't seem to chart well. That all changed with *Dark Side of the Moon*. According to the Rock and Roll Hall of Fame,

> **"the album signaled rock's willingness to move from adolescence into adulthood, conceptually addressing such subjects as aging, madness, money and time. From its prismatic cover artwork to the music therein, *Dark Side of the Moon* is a classic-rock milestone."**

The album was released in 1973 and shot up the charts in both Britain and the United States. On April 28, the album reached #1 in the United States, Pink Floyd's first U.S. #1; it only got as high as #2 in Britain. It stayed on the U.S. Top-200 album charts for 741 weeks, including 591 consecutive weeks from 1976 to 1988! More than 15 million copies of the album were sold in the United States alone. The album's "Money" cracked the U.S. Top-20 singles chart at #13, the first time Pink Floyd had a hit single in the United States.

The group followed up *Dark Side* with *Wish You Were Here*. With these two albums, it seemed as though Syd had finally been purged from the group. Whereas the styles of the remaining members had seemed somewhat helter-skelter in the group's early post-Syd days, things seemed to have finally come together in these albums.

The Covers

Dark Side of the Moon also brought attention to the group's album covers. They were not ordinary album covers; these were works of art. Beginning with *A Saucerful of Secrets*, the albums were designed by Hipgnosis, a design team composed of Storm Thorgerson and Aubrey "Po" Powell, former roommates of Syd's. According to Storm, the design team tries to design covers that reflect the band's music:

> **"Pink Floyd's music is very evocative. . . . They conjure up very unusual atmospheres of feelings and spaces. When we're doing the packaging, we're trying in part to say this represents the music or the band in pictorial or graphic terms."**

It could never be said that the members of Pink Floyd didn't put their all into their performances, as shown by this photograph taken of Roger during a performance. Hipgnosis, a design team, also tried to draw from that emotion and the group's music when creating Pink Floyd's album covers.

For *Dark Side*, Storm drew the sound wave of a heartbeat. According to him:

> **"If the album is about any one thing, possibly it's madness . . . irrationality, the other side of one's life. . . . They had people discussing these mad little bits about their lives, and they used the heartbeat as a rhythm underneath it."**

Some of the album covers have even become collectors' items.

Climbing *The Wall*

In 1979, Pink Floyd released what is undoubtedly its most famous album, *The Wall*. This was Roger's baby. It was his idea. In an interview with a BBC radio DJ, Roger described how he came up with the idea:

> **"Well, the idea for 'The Wall' came from ten years of touring, rock shows, I think, particularly the last few years in '75 and in '77 we were playing to very large audiences, some of whom were our old audience who'd come to see us play, but most of whom were only there for the beer, in big stadiums, and, er, consequently it became rather an alienating experience doing the shows. I became very conscious of a wall between us and our audience and so this record started out as being an expression of those feelings."**

Roger also admitted that some of the inspiration for the rock opera came from his own life, especially his childhood. As a very young boy, Roger lost his father in a war. His school career was also less than happy. Those two incidents find their way into *The Wall*. The production is about loss.

The Wall hit the #1 spot on U.S. charts and stayed there for fifteen weeks. That was better than it did in Britain, where it only reached #3. As of December 2006, it had been certified **platinum** twenty-three times in the United States alone. "Another Brick in the Wall" was the album's breakout single, and it stayed at the top of the singles charts

With *The Wall*, Pink Floyd really hit it big. Drawn from life, the rock opera finally brought the group to the #1 spot on U.S. charts. The rock opera's "characters" are even featured at the Rock and Roll Hall of Fame in Cleveland, Ohio. Pink Floyd has performed the rock opera twenty-four times, the last more than twenty-five years ago.

for four weeks. The group performed the rock opera twenty-four times, the last time being on June 17, 1981, in Germany.

With the success of the album and subsequent performances, you would have thought things were going well for the group.

Not true.

Pink Floyd Hits the Wall

Because it was his idea, Roger controlled almost everything associated with *The Wall*, as well some things that weren't connected with that album. Roger was assuming much of the artistic control of the group and its music, and this didn't sit well with his bandmates. They were artists as well, and some began to feel their creativity being stifled. This led to some major conflicts between Roger and other members of the group. But according to Rick, in-fighting wasn't anything new for the group:

"We fought during 'The Wall,' which was an album Waters wrote, based on his family story, we clashed long before that, during the period of the *Dark Side* and 'Wish You Were Here.' Actually, we never got along."

Though the group found musical success with *The Wall*, the album brought simmering tensions among group members to the surface. Other members thought Roger was taking over the musical direction of the group, and they didn't like it. Perhaps they felt as though they were banging their heads against the wall to have their ideas heard!

During the recording of the album, Rick was fired. For him, however, that turned out not to be a bad thing, especially when the band hired him to perform for a set fee at *The Wall* concerts. It was very expensive to perform *The Wall* live. Rick's fee was guaranteed, but the others had to make up any monetary shortfall themselves. So Rick was the only one who actually made any money from the performances.

The film *Pink Floyd: The Wall* was written by Roger and released in 1982. Though it contained the music from the album, most of the songs had been re-recorded by Bob Geldof. Critically it received mediocre reviews, but fans loved it.

The Final Cut of Pink Floyd

Bad feelings between group members only got worse after *The Wall* was released. Fights between Roger and David became so bad that they reportedly never appeared at the studio together when the group's next album, *The Final Cut*, was recorded.

Released in 1983, the album is dedicated to the memory of Roger's father. The split within the band was apparent, even on the album cover. The album is listed as being "by Roger Waters, performed by Pink Floyd: Roger Waters, David Gilmour, Nick Mason." It was not a big hit with the fans, though the critics generally gave it good reviews.

The group didn't tour for this album, and not long after its release, Pink Floyd unofficially called it quits. Two years later, Roger sent Columbia and EMI Records formal notice that he was no longer associated with Pink Floyd.

Despite a lawsuit asking them not to perform as Pink Floyd, Nick and David continued to record as Pink Floyd. Their first album was *A Momentary Lapse of Reason*, released in 1987. For the first time in the group's career, the band relied on outside songwriters to provide the content for the album. This album also saw Rick's return, again as a salaried employee.

In 1994, *The Division Bell* became the group's fourth #1 album. Rick was reinstated as a full Pink Floyd member for this album, and he wrote a significant amount of the material featured on the album. A year later, *P*u*l*s*e* became Pink Floyd's fifth #1 album. The group's membership might not be the same, but Pink Floyd still had lots of fans.

Pink Floyd at the Waldorf-Astoria! Who would have thought it possible? Well, anyone paying attention to the rock world would have known that it was a given that the group would make it into the Rock and Roll Hall of Fame. In 1995, David, Rick, and Nick (from left) accepted the award.

The Hall of Fame Calls

January 16, 1996, was a big night for Pink Floyd. Almost thirty years after the release of its first album, the group was being inducted into the Rock and Roll Hall of Fame. Syd, David, Nick, Roger, and Rick were taking their places among the other giants of the rock world.

Among the others being inducted that evening during the glamorous ceremonies at New York City's Waldorf-Astoria Hotel were Gladys Knight and the Pips, the Velvet Underground, the Shirelles, Pete Seeger, Jefferson Airplane, and David Bowie. All of them had met the tough standards the nominating committee of the Rock and Roll Hall of Fame required just to put a musician's name on the ballot. According to Rock and Roll Hall of Fame rules, twenty-five years must have passed since a potential nominee's first recording. Those considered for nomination must have made a significant contribution to the development of rock music. Those who meet the criteria are placed on the ballot, which is sent to music experts all over the world. To be inducted, the nominee must have the most votes, and be selected on more than 50 percent of the ballots.

Smashing Pumpkins' Billy Corgan presented Pink Floyd at the induction ceremony, calling the group the "ultimate rock and roll **anomaly**." Rick, David, and Nick were there in person to accept their awards, and after the presentation, Billy joined them for a performance of "Wish You Were Here."

Visitors to Cleveland's Rock and Roll Hall of Fame Museum will find Pink Floyd's display on the sixth floor. Just two floors down, however, is another Pink Floyd—well, at least a Roger Waters—contribution to the museum.

The Wall at the Hall

Even before Pink Floyd was nominated for inclusion in the Rock and Roll Hall of Fame, even before the facility was constructed, Roger had made a significant contribution to the museum. After a discussion with the museum's chief curator, Roger helped put together an exhibition about *The Wall*. According to the curator,

> **The entire exhibit is about 38 feet long and 22 feet tall. The depth of The Wall is 2 feet. The teacher is 28 feet in length.**

The exhibit is animated. Teacher's eyes light up and he moves as visitors hear a voice from the Wall say:

> **If you don't eat your meat, you won't have any pudding. How can you have any pudding if you don't eat your meat?**

Roger lets the audience in on how he came up with *The Wall* in a letter on view along with the exhibit:

> **In the old days, pre-*Dark Side of the Moon*, Pink Floyd played to audiences which, by virtue of their size allowed an intimacy of connection that was magical. However, success overtook us and by 1977**

Roger helped bring his *Wall* to the Rock and Roll Hall of Fame. The exhibition features the Wall and the teacher, and is thirty-eight feet long and twenty-two feet high. Visitors to the exhibit can read a letter Roger wrote telling about what inspired him to compose one of the most famous rock operas in history.

we were playing in football stadiums. The magic crushed beneath the weight of numbers, we were becoming addicted to the trappings of popularity. I found myself increasingly alienated in that atmosphere of avarice and ego until one night in the Olympic Stadium, Montreal. Some crazed teenage fan was clawing his way up the storm netting that separated us from the human cattle pen in front of the stage, screaming his devotion to the 'demi-gods' beyond his reach. Incensed by his misunderstanding and my own connivance, I spat my frustration in his face. Later that night, back at the hotel, shocked by my behavior, I was faced with a choice. To deny my addiction and embrace that 'comfortably numb' but 'magic-less' existence or accept the burden of insight, take the road less traveled and embark on the often-painful journey to discover who I was and where I fit. The Wall was the picture I drew for myself to help me make that choice. **"**

Remastered and Re-Released

The early twenty-first century brought new sounds from Pink Floyd. Well, perhaps not entirely new. The group was still popular, and record executives decided to take advantage of that popularity. According to Rick:

"The fact that people still know us is, in my opinion, a result of our music and of the big money that runs the music industry today. The people who control the industry are accountants who recycle everything in new, nostalgic packages, and everything else, to make more money.**"**

The "recycling" was successful. In 2000, a live version of *The Wall* was released as *Is There Anybody Out There? The Wall Live 1980–81*. The album was a compilation of concerts the group had performed in

Rick, Nick, and David (left to right) have spent much of the early new century in the recording studio. New recordings by the now mostly Roger-less group piqued the interest in Pink Floyd's older recordings, and the guys helped remaster and re-release some of its early work. This brought them new fans.

London between 1980 and 1981. The album reached #1 on *Billboard*'s Internet Album Sales charts.

Roger rejoined David, Nick, and Rick for *Echoes*, released in 2001. *Echoes* featured Pink Floyd's most popular tracks—but not everyone liked the album. There seemed to be no rhyme or reason for how the songs appeared on the two-disc set. They are not presented by year of release, or even of writing. Some reviewers have criticized the project because, heard outside the context of the album on which they appeared, the songs included on *Echoes* lose some of their power. Another criticism arose because some of the songs on *Echoes*, including "Shine On You Crazy Diamond" and "Marooned," have been drastically edited. Still, *Echoes* reached #2 on U.S. album charts.

In 2003, *The Dark Side of the Moon* was released in a special thirtieth-anniversary edition. The CD took advantage of the newest high-tech innovations, including high-res surround sound. Even the cover was redone for this special project. In a blast from the past, a special vinyl version—something called a "record"—of *The Dark Side of the Moon* was released the same year. In 2004, *The Final Cut* was re-released with an extra song. Plans were also underway for a special release of *Wish You Were Here*.

Alone

Besides performing as part of Pink Floyd, David, Nick, and Rick have been involved in other projects. Roger has also been busy since his Pink Floyd days.

David has taken on several projects, not all of them music related. Musically, however, he headlined the 2004 Wembley concert that celebrated the fiftieth anniversary of the Fender Stratocaster guitar. Readers of *Guitarist* magazine also voted him the Best Fender Guitar Player Ever, outpolling such legends as Jimi Hendrix and Eric Clapton. He released a solo album, *On an Island*, in 2006. The album debuted on British charts at #1 and was certified platinum in several countries, including Canada and Poland. The album's release was followed by a tour of Europe, Canada, and the United States, with Rick in his band. Nick joined them for a special performance of "Wish You Were Here" and "Comfortably Numb" at the Royal Albert Hall.

David has become a well-known **philanthropist** as well. In 2003, he sold his home in London and donated the proceeds to Crisis, a charity that assists the homeless. When Pink Floyd interest increased after the group's performance at Live 8, David announced that he would donate profits from post–Live 8 sales to charity. He is also active in the European Union Mental Health and Illness Association, Emergency, Greenpeace, Amnesty International, the Lung Foundation, Nordoff-Robbins Music Therapy, PETA, and several groups fighting global warming. In November 2003, he was made a Commander of the British Empire (CBE) for his philanthropic work and his contributions to music.

Nick has continued performing and producing, but most of his time has been spent on two projects—writing a book and participating in auto racing. In 2005, *Inside Out: A Personal History of Pink Floyd* was released. Nick admits that the tale he tells is rather one-sided (his view on things), but some reviewers commented on the book's humorous side, calling it an interesting look at a band many people thought of

David's work as a guitarist earned him the Best Fender Guitar Player award by readers of *Guitarist*. His solo projects have been successful as well. But perhaps his biggest contribution to the world is as a philanthropist. His charity work and musical contributions even led to a knightship by Queen Elizabeth II in 2003.

One of Nick's biggest loves is auto racing. He's a huge fan for sure, but he's also a participant as an auto racer and race team owner. He also wrote a tell-all book about his days with Pink Floyd. Nick admits it's one-sided, but critics have praised the book for its humorous look at life with the group.

as always being in a depressed mood. A huge auto racing fan, Nick has participated in the 24 hours at Le Mans. His company Ten Tenths owns and races several classic cars.

After leaving Pink Floyd, Roger released some solo albums, but never achieved the acclaim he had received as part of Pink Floyd. He also organized and participated in a charity concert in 1990 that commemorated the dismantling of the Berlin Wall the previous year. In 2004, he released two tracks on the Internet inspired by the U.S.

invasion of Iraq. Though the songs were written shortly after the invasion, Roger has stated in numerous interviews that he waited to release them until just before the 2004 presidential election in hope that they would help defeat President George W. Bush's reelection bid. In 2005, Roger joined Eric Clapton for a special performance of "Wish You Were Here" for the NBC benefit concert for tsunami relief.

But Roger's biggest project was perhaps the one that took the longest. In September 2005, Roger released *Ça Ira*, an opera in French. The project took sixteen years to complete and features a full orchestra.

Rick was always the quiet member of Pink Floyd, and he has remained generally out of the spotlight. He has released some solo projects and performed with David on his *On an Island* album and tour.

Sadly, the last of the original Pink Floyd members, Syd Barrett, died in 2006. After leaving the group, Syd became increasingly secluded until he was rarely seen in public. Still, the other members of the group never forgot the important role Syd played in helping the band find its way in the sometimes convoluted world of rock music.

Reunion?

It seems as though as soon as a big-name band splits up, rumors begin to circulate about when the group will get back together. The bigger the band, the more rumors that circulate. This has certainly been true with Pink Floyd, especially whenever two or more members are seen representing the group.

In November 2005, Pink Floyd was inducted into the UK Music Hall of Fame. David and Nick accepted the award in person. Roger appeared via a video hook-up from Rome, where he was in rehearsals with *Ça Ira*. Rick couldn't attend because he was hospitalized for cataract surgery. Although only two band members were in the same place, many saw Roger's participation as a hopeful sign of a possible reunion.

The rumor mill went into overtime after the group's Live 8 London performance. There was certainly an increased interest in the group; British record store HMV reported that sales of *Echoes* increased 1343 percent the week following Pink Floyd's performance. Amazon.co.uk, the U.K.'s version of the American Amazon.com, reported skyrocketing sales of *The Wall* (up 3600 percent) and *Wish You Were Here* (an increase of 2000 percent) as well. According

Will Pink Floyd ever reunite? Fans take hope from the appearance of the group—including Roger—at events such as Live 8. So far, there's no indication that the group will get back together, but all hope is not lost. Some of the band members have said they'd perform as a complete group for a worthy cause.

to the Italian newspaper *La Repubblica*, a promoter even offered the group $250 million for a world tour. The group declined.

It would take more than money to bring the group together again. After all, the dispute between David and Roger was very real—and very nasty. In an interview with *Compact Disc* magazine, David says of Roger:

    "He had developed his own limited, or very simple style. He was never very keen on improving himself as a bass player and half the time I would play bass

on the records because I would tend to do it quicker. Right back to those early records; I mean, at least half the bass on all recorded output is me anyway. . . . Rog used to come in and say—'Thank you very much'—to me once in a while for winning him bass-playing polls.

In a February 2006 interview in *La Repubblica*, David said he agreed to participate in Live 8 because it was a good cause, and he wanted to make peace with Roger. Again hopes were raised. Nick has been quoted in the same newspaper that Pink Floyd would be willing to reunite for a concert "that would support Israeli–Palestinian peace efforts." So Rick's claim that "Pink Floyd is like a marriage that's on a permanent trial separation," doesn't mean the divorce papers have been signed: the door hasn't been closed on a possible reunion on behalf of a good cause.

Fans grab any glimmer of hope they can find that Pink Floyd will reunite—perhaps for a tour or a CD in honor of Syd. In the meantime, they'll have to be content with what is available. And fortunately, there's plenty good stuff available!

1964 Bob Klose, Roger Waters, Nick Mason, and Rick Wright form the band that will become Pink Floyd.

1965 Syd Barrett joins the group.

Roger, Rick, Nick, Bob, and Syd play a gig as Pink Floyd for the first time.

Bob leaves the band.

1966 **February** Pink Floyd play a series of happenings at the Marquee Club.

September The group begins its association with the underground newspaper the *International Times*.

December Pink Floyd plays the first of many concerts at London's UFO Club.

1967 Pink Floyd cuts its first single.

Pink Floyd tours with American superstar Jimi Hendrix.

January The group lays down tracks for the film *Tonite Let's All Make Love in London*.

April 5 Pink Floyd's debut album is released.

April 29–30 Pink Floyd plays at a fund-raising event at the prestigious Alexandra Palace in London.

May The group performs at the Games for May concert in London.

May 14 Pink Floyd appears on British television for the first time.

October Pink Floyd comes to the United States for the first time.

1968 *A Saucerful of Secrets* is released and is the only Pink Floyd album that does not chart in the United States.

January David Gilmour joins the band.

April 6 Pink Floyd announces that Syd is leaving the group.

1973 **June 17** *Dark Side of the Moon* is released and becomes #1 in the United States.

1979 *The Wall* is released.

1981 Roger appears with Pink Floyd for the last time before leaving the group.

June 17 Pink Floyd performs *The Wall* for the last time.

1982 The film *Pink Floyd: The Wall* is released.

1985 Roger notifies the group's record companies that he is no longer associated with Pink Floyd.

1987 Pink Floyd releases its first post-Roger album, *A Momentary Lapse of Reason*.

1994 *The Division Bell* becomes the group's fourth #1 album.

1995 *P*U*L*S*E* becomes the group's fifth #1 album.

1996 **January 16** Pink Floyd is inducted into the Rock and Roll Hall of Fame.

2005 **November** Pink Floyd is inducted into the UK Music Hall of Fame.

July 2 Pink Floyd, with Roger, performs at Live 8.

2006 **July 7** Syd Barrett dies.

Albums

1967 *The Piper at the Gates of Dawn*

1968 *A Saucerful of Secrets*

1969 *Music from the Film More*
Ummagumma

1970 *Atom Heart Mother*
Meddle

1971 *Relics*

1972 *Obscured by Clouds*

1973 *A Nice Pair*
The Dark Side of the Moon

1975 *Wish You Were Here*

1977 *Animals*

1979 *The Wall*

1981 *A Collection of Great Dance Songs*

1983 *The Final Cut*
Works

1987 *A Momentary Lapse of Reason*

1988 *Delicate Sound of Thunder*

1992 *Shine On*

1994 *The Division Bell*

1995 *P*U*L*S*E*

2000 *Is There Anybody Out There?*

2001 *Echoes: The Best of Pink Floyd*

Number-One Singles

1979 "Another Brick in the Wall, Part II"

1980 "Comfortably Numb"
"Hey You"

1987 "Learning to Fly"
"On the Turning Away"

1994 "Keep Talking"

Select Videos

1970 *Pink Floyd Live—St. Tropez*

1989 *Live in Venice*

2003 *Live at Pompeii*

2004 *The Pink Floyd and Syd Barrett Story*

2005 *Inside Pink Floyd: A Critical Review 1967–1996*
London 1966–1967
Pink Floyd: Making of the Dark Side of the Moon
The Wall 25th Anniversary Edition

2006 *On the Rock Trail: Pink Floyd*
Pink Floyd's Landmark Albums
Pulse
Reflections and Echoes
Shine On

2007 *Pink Floyd: Up Close and Personal*
Rock Milestones: The Wall

Film

1982 *Pink Floyd: The Wall*

Awards and Recognition

1973 Grammy Awards: Album of the Year (nomination, *Dark Side of the Moon*).

1980 Grammy Awards: Album of the Year (nomination, *The Wall*), Best Rock Performance by Duo or Group (nomination, "Another Brick in the Wall, Part II); awarded a Silver Clef for charity work for The Nordoff-Robbins Music Center.

1983 BAFTA: Best Original Song ("Another Brick in the Wall"), Best Sound (*The Wall*).

1994 Grammy Awards: Best Rock Instrumental Performance ("Marooned").

1996 Pink Floyd is inducted into the Rock and Roll Hall of Fame.

2005 Pink Floyd is inducted into the UK Music Hall of Fame.

Books

Bench, Jeff, and Daniel O'Brien. *Pink Floyd's The Wall: In the Studio, on Stage, and on Screen.* Richmond, Surrey, U.K.: Reynolds & Hearn, 2004.

Fitch, Vernon. *Pink Floyd Encyclopedia.* Burlington, Ont.: Collector's Guide Publishing, 2005.

Harris, John. *The Dark Side of the Moon: The Making of Pink Floyd's Masterpiece.* New York: Plenum, 2005.

Mason, Nick. *Inside Out: A Personal History of Pink Floyd.* San Francisco, Calif.: Chronicle Books, 2005.

Rose, Philip. *Which One's Pink?* Burlington, Ont.: Collector's Guide Publishing, 2000.

Thorgerson, Storm, and Peter Curzon. *Mind Over Matter: The Images of Pink Floyd.* London: Sanctuary Publishing, 2003.

Watkinson, Mike, and Pete Anderson. *Syd Barrett: Crazy Diamond— The Dawn of Pink Floyd.* London: Omnibus Press, 2007.

Willis, Tim. *Madcap: The Half-Life of Syd Barrett, Pink Floyd's Lost Genius.* London: Short Books Ltd., 2002.

Web Sites

www.ca-ira.com
Roger Waters

www.davidgilmour.com
David Gilmour

www.pinkfloyd.com/home/home.html
Pink Floyd

www.rockhall.com
Rock and Roll Hall of Fame

www.sonymusic.com/artists/PinkFloyd
Pink Floyd on Sony

anomaly—Something that is different from the norm or the expected.

bootleg—An illegally made product.

cannabis—A drug produced in various forms (the best known is marijuana) from the dried leaves and flowers of the hemp plant.

counterculture—A culture that has ideas and behaviors that are consciously and deliberately very different from those of the larger society.

cross-dresser—Someone who dresses in the clothing of members of the opposite sex.

genre—One of the categories that artistic works of all kinds can be divided into on the basis of form, style, or subject matter.

homage—A show of reverence and respect toward someone.

liner notes—Printed information about a recording that appears on the cover or as part of the packaging.

mescaline—A drug that produces hallucinations that is extracted from the button-shaped nodules on the stem of the peyote.

mesmerize—To absorb all of somebody's attention.

philanthropist—Someone who improves the material, social, and spiritual welfare of humanity.

platinum—A status that signifies that an album or CD has sold two million copies or a single has sold one million.

synonymous—Meaning the same or almost the same as something else.

third-world—A group of countries that are less economically advanced.

underground—A group that is separate from the main social or artistic environment.

venue—Location of event.

Herman Edward is a writer in Upstate New York, who shares his home with a variety of cat friends. He has a special affection for Pink Floyd, since his father, Floyd, was nicknamed Pinky in the group's honor.

Picture Credits